MEDIEVAL WELSH
MONASTERIES

Author
John W. Roberts

Translated by
Gareth Williams

Cardiff
University of Wales Press
1987

British Library Cataloguing in Publication Data

Roberts, John W.
  Medieval Welsh monasteries.
  1. Monasteries — Wales — History
  I. Title   II. Y Mynachlogydd yn yr oesoedd
canol. *English*
  271'.009429   BX2603

  ISBN 0-7083-0961-5

ACKNOWLEDGEMENTS

The publishers would like to thank the following for
permission to reproduce photographs and for their
assistance.

Aerofilms Ltd: 1(A)

Cadw, Welsh Historic Monuments: 1(B), 4(E), 4(F),
  5(H), 11(B)

John B. Hilling: 2(C)

National Monuments Record for Wales: 4(G)

Italian State Tourist Office, London: 8(D)

The British Library: 8(A), 8(E), 9(G), 12(D), 15(Q)

Commissioners of Public Works, Ireland: 8(C)

BBC Hulton Picture Library: 9(I), 10(L), 11(C), 21(E)

The Mansell Collection Limited: 10(J)

A. F. Kersting: 12(F)

English Heritage: 12(H), 14(L), 23(M)

Royal Commission on the Historical Monuments of
  England: 13(I)

Lynne Sieger: 14(N), 15(O), 16(V), 22(K), 23(L)

Oxfordshire County Libraries: 15(R)

Entwistle Photographic Services: 16(T)

Eric Hall: 20(A)

Dean of Worcester Cathedral, (Photographer: J. R.
  Thoumine): 22(J) (top photograph)

Trustees of the Victoria and Albert Museum: 22(J)
  (bottom photograph)

CONTENTS

This book is based on an original Welsh title, *Y
Mynachlogydd yng Nghymru.*

Printed in Wales by Graham Harcourt (Printers) Ltd.,
Swansea.

1. RUINS AND REMAINS

Remains like those in photographs Ⓐ and Ⓑ are to be seen in many parts of England and Wales. Thousands of people visit them every year, and they will continue to attract tourists and sight-seers because of their grandeur, great age and imposing size. You can appreciate why historians from all over the world are fascinated by the kind of ruins shown here, namely Rievaulx in Yorkshire Ⓐ and Tintern in Gwent Ⓑ.

By looking carefully you will realize that these pictures were taken from the air. What kind of buildings do you see? It is difficult to be absolutely sure, but both photographs seem to show a building that might have been a church, as well as the remains of other, smaller buildings of a different kind. Such remains can tell us a great deal; or, to be more precise, they tell archaeologists and architects a great deal, because they have the expert knowledge which enables them to make sense and draw plans of these buildings. Here is one such plan: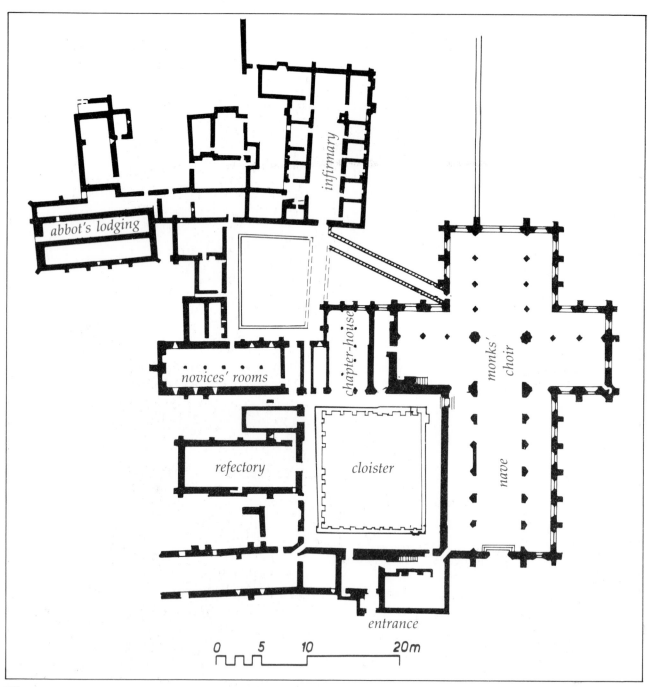

infirmary

abbot's lodging

chapter-house

monks' choir

novices' rooms

nave

refectory

cloister

entrance

0   5   10   20m

Looking at it, you will have been struck by two things in particular. One is that the largest single building in it is the church, so this must be a religious institution of some kind. Secondly, the number and purpose of other buildings such as the **refectory**, the infirmary, the **walks** and the **novices'** rooms suggest that this was where a community of people used to live together. It is in fact the plan of a **monastery**, which can be described as a community of **monks** or **nuns** who have chosen to live together with the main aim of worshipping God in accordance with the rules of the order to which they belong.

Are there any monastic ruins in your locality or within reach of your school? As a guide, look at map which shows you where the most important monastic remains can be found in Wales.

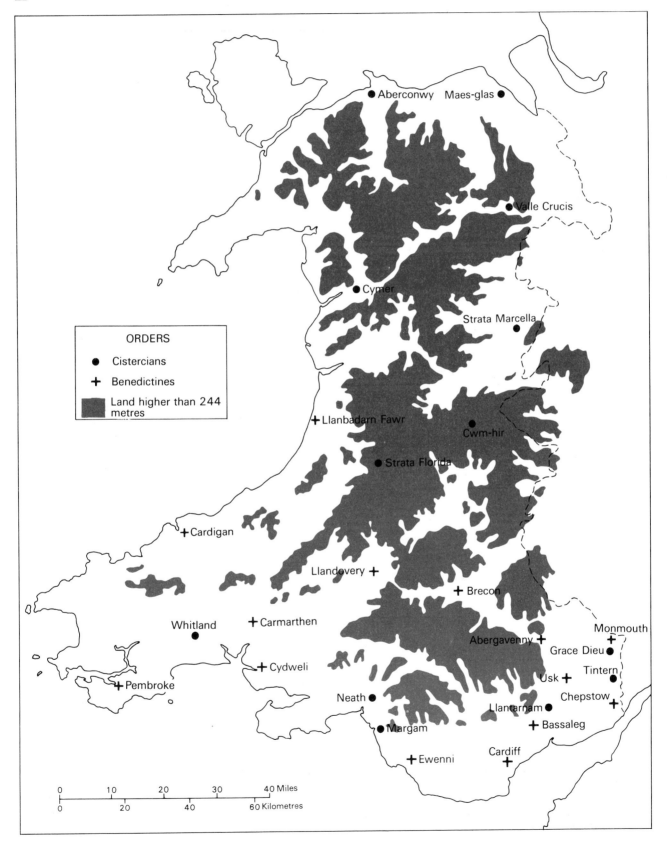

ORDERS

● Cistercians

✚ Benedictines

▓ Land higher than 244 metres

Does anything strike you about the location and distribution of these monastic sites? In what parts of the country are most of them to be found? From your knowledge of Welsh history and geography, what monasteries were possibly linked with towns or castles? Would you say they are located in remote or inaccessible places? What other questions might be asked? See if you can draw up a table listing your own observations and conclusions.

E West window of Tintern Abbey.

There is always something to be learned from ruins like those shown here. What would you say is striking about them?

Fortunately, thanks to the studies carried out by experts in this field, we are beginning to have a much fuller picture of buildings whose only remaining traces today are their ruins.

F Door of Valle Crucis Abbey.

G West door of Strata Florida.

4

An artist's impression of Tintern Abbey as it once was by Alan Sorrell.

Picture H is a reconstruction by a well-known artist of Tintern Abbey and its buildings as they might have looked centuries ago.

At that time there were literally hundreds of monasteries throughout Wales and England, though only a handful still remain. Many historic ones have disappeared entirely, while in some places only the occasional local name serves as a reminder of where a monastery had once existed. In other places, though, imposing ruins still stand, silent and brooding, and in the following pages we will try to penetrate the veil of secrecy that shrouds them in order to find out what the monks and their monasteries were like at their peak.

2. FOUNDATIONS

How do we find out about the beginnings of the monasteries and their subsequent growth? One particularly rich source that the historian utilizes is that provided by contemporary manuscripts and documents, or very old copies of them in libraries and museums. One of the most important manuscripts for Welsh historians is *Brut y Tywysogion* (The Chronicle of the Princes), which relates events in the history of Wales from the time of Cadwaladr ap Cadwallon who died, according to the *Chronicle*, in 681 or 682, to the death of Llywelyn ap Gruffudd, the last native Prince of Wales, in 1282. Uncertainty still exists as to the actual authorship of the manuscript but historians believe that it was compiled at the monastery of Strata Florida in Ceredigion in Dyfed, basing this conclusion on the fact that it is frequently referred to in the course of the *Chronicle*.

Various copies of the *Chronicle* have survived, and scholars have translated and published them. Here are several excerpts from one version, translated from the original Latin, all of which contain references to the monastery at Strata Florida:
A

A

1164   In that year, through the will of God and at the instigation of the Holy Spirit, a community of monks came to the place called Strata Florida ...

1185 ... In that year died Dafydd, abbot of Strata Florida ...

1186 ... In that year, about the month of July, a community of monks went from Strata Florida to Rhedynog Felen in Gwynedd. And then died Peter, abbot of Clairvaux.

1191 ... And Owain ap Rhys died at Strata Florida.

1201 ... In that year the community of Strata Florida went to the new church on the eve of Whit Sunday after it had been nobly and handsomely built ... and in that year died Gruffudd ... son to the Lord Rhys and a prince of Wales by right and inheritance, after assuming the habit of the Order at Strata Florida, and there he was honourably buried.

1204 A year after that, Hywel son of Lord Rhys the Great was slain in Cemmaes through treachery by the men of Maelgwn his brother; and he died after he had assumed the habit of the Order of Strata Florida, and he was honourably buried in the same grave as Gruffudd his brother ...

These are some of the many references in the *Chronicle* to the **abbey**. To what extent is it possible to write an outline of the history of Strata Florida between 1164 and 1204? What facts clearly emerge? This is not easy, since there are so few facts in the *Chronicle*. But there is another important document dating from this period, the charter of Rhys ap Gruffudd, which provides further information about Strata Florida: B

B Be it known to all that I, Rhys, Prince of South Wales, have begun the task of building the venerable abbey called Strat-flur [Strata Florida]; since its inception I have loved and cherished it, increased its estates and possessions and enlarged them as much as I could with the assistance of the Lord, granting to it with a devout mind for the cure of my soul and the souls of my predecessors and successors, pasture, arable and mountain land for the grazing of animals, as much as was fitting; and the same gift which I have conferred on the said monastery I confirm again in this year of 1184 ... Also, my three sons, Gruffudd, Rhys and Maredudd have at the same time, in the same place, conferred the same gift upon the abbot of Strat-fflur ...

This charter has led some historians into believing that it was Rhys ap Gruffudd who founded the abbey in 1184. But you notice from the *Chronicle* that the date given there for the foundation does not correspond to that in the charter. Apparently there exists another charter which shows that the land on the banks of the River Fflur in Ceredigion was a gift from the Norman Robert Fitz Stephen. Twelve

monks from the monastery at Whitland arrived in 1164 to found the new abbey on this piece of land, though in 1180 the abbey moved to the banks of the Teifi. The original site is therefore referred to as 'The Old Monastery' (*Hen Fynachlog*).

With this added information, you should be able to answer the following questions:

1. What do we know about the founding of Strata Florida?

2. Who were the abbey's principal **patrons**?

3. Can you name one of the abbots of the early period?

4. What links did the princes of Wales have with the monastery?

You noticed that it was monks from the abbey at Whitland who founded Strata Florida in 1164, but how had they arrived in Whitland in the first place? The answer is that they came from the monastery of Clairvaux in France, which therefore became the mother-house of Whitland abbey just as Whitland became the mother-house of Strata Florida. The **patron** was the person who gave the land on which the monks could found a new monastery. We could find evidence of this kind for every single one of the monasteries indicated on the map of Wales (page 3 D). The following table C tabulates some of the facts relating to several of the larger Welsh monasteries.

C

Monastery	Patron	Mother-house	Date
Brecon	Bernard of Neufmarché	Battle	about 1110
Cardiff	Robert Fitz Hamon	Tewkesbury	1106
Carmarthen	Henry I	Battle	about 1110
Chepstow	William Fitzosbern	Cormeilles (France)	1071
Cydweli	Roger, bishop of Salisbury	Sherborne	1114
Ewenni	Maurice of London	Gloucester	1141
Llanbadarn Fawr	Gilbert Fitz Richard	Gloucester	1116-7
Pembroke	Arnulf of Montgomery	St Martin, Séez (France)	about 1098

1. What do those listed as Patrons in the table have in common?

2. What name do we give the period in which these monasteries were founded? In which centuries were they established?

3. Look at map on page 3. What do the Benedictine sites have in common?

4. What does the term 'mother-house' mean?

Each of the Welsh monasteries listed in table C had a mother-house in either England or Normandy. Furthermore, they all belonged to the Benedictine Order of monks, an order which received considerable support from the Normans. Following their successful military incursion into South Wales, the Norman barons greatly favoured this particular order with many gifts of land.

The next table D gives details of eight monasteries belonging to the Cistercian Order.

D

Monastery	Patron	Mother-house	Date
Whitland	John of Torrington	Clairvaux (France)	1140
Cwm-hir	Cadwallon ap Madog	Whitland	1176
Strata Florida	Rhys ap Gruffudd	Whitland	1184
Strata Marcella	Owain Cyfeiliog	Whitland	1170
Llantarnam	Hywel ap Iorwerth	Strata Florida	about 1179
Aberconwy	Llywelyn the Great	Strata Florida	1186
Cymer	Llywelyn the Great	Cwm-hir	1199
Valle Crucis	Madog ap Gruffudd	Strata Marcella	1200

1. Is there anything particularly noteworthy about the mother-houses of these monasteries?

2. Why, in your opinion, were three new monasteries founded by the monks of Whitland and another two by the monks of Strata Florida?

3. Do you notice any striking differences between tables C and D?

Here is an example of a gift to one of the monasteries referred to in table D above: E

E **A GIFT TO THE ABBEY OF STRATA MARCELLA, 1201**

Be it known to all sons present and future of Holy Mother Church that I, Wenwynwyn, the son of Owain Cyfeiliog, have given to God and the glorious Virgin Mother and the monks of Strata Marcella for the health of my soul in free and perpetual gift all the pastures of the whole province which is called Cyfeiliog within those boundaries, namely, from Afon Maenmelyn as far as Llwyn y Groes and from there in a direct line as far as Blaen Nant Hanog, and from there by Nant Hanog as far as its mouth, then as far as Abernant ... and along that rivulet to its source, and from there to Carneddwen and thence to Gobleidde, and from Pen Gobleidde ... to its mouth and then via Bache to Aber Dyfyngwm, and thence along the Dyfyngwm to its source ...

The Cistercian Order was supported by the Normans, too, to a certain extent, and Norman patrons helped found some Cistercian monasteries in South Wales, as is shown in table F:

F

Monastery	Patron	Mother-house	Date
Grace Dieu	John of Monmouth	Dore (Herefordshire)	1226
Margam	Robert, earl of Gloucester	Clairvaux (France)	1147
Neath	Richard de Granville	Savigny (France)	1130
Tintern	Walter Fitz Richard	L'Aumône (France)	1131

To which of the above abbeys was the following gift made? G

G I, Philip, Lord of Marcoss have given to God and the Blessed Mary and the monks of Neath, for the good of my soul and the sould of my predecessors and successors, fourteen acres of arable land of my estate at Marcross ...

C A hermit's cell, Great Skellig, Ireland.

A

In picture A you see a young man kneeling in front of an abbot, who is cutting the young man's hair very short. When he has done so, another monk will shave the crown of the head until he has made a circle known as a **tonsure**. This is an indication that the young man is being received as a **novice** and as such he will be required to take the following oath:

B

B I am taking leave of my parents, my brother and kinfolk and parting with all my earthly goods and the vain glories of this world. I am turning away from the desires of my own will to let God's will be done. I accept all the hardships of monastic life and vow to be poor, chaste and obedient in the hope of attaining heaven. I vow also steadfastly to abide in this monastery all the days of my life.

Here therefore is a young man solemnly undertaking to devote his life to prayer and to work on God's behalf, and to live in a monastery for the rest of his years. Young women took this step too. Since Roman times there have been people in Europe who have sought to withdraw from the problems of this world and chosen to live the life of a **hermit** in a retreat, or cell.

Sometimes a group of men would come together to establish a community of hermits or a monastery. One of the most famous monasteries of this early period was that of St Benedict, founded on Monte Cassino in Italy in 525. See picture D.

E St Benedict.

Benedict was a nobleman's son living in Italy in the sixth century who gave up his comfortable life in order to become a monk.

D Monte Cassino as it is today.

Benedict decided to draw up a set of rules according to which monks might live, and they were so successful that many monasteries were built throughout Europe where the monks lived according to the Rule of Benedict. This was how the **Benedictine** Order originated. The Rule of Benedict required a monk to take the following vow: F

F I accept all the hardships of monastic life. I vow to be poor, chaste and obedient in the hope of attaining heaven. I vow steadfastly to abide in this monastery all the days of my life.

St Benedict divided the monastic day into three parts:

1. The hours of prayer
2. The hours of study
3. The hours of work

This meant that every day of the week eight hours a day were devoted to prayer and seven hours to the work of maintaining the monastery, though on Sunday the whole day was spent in worship.

It was communities such as these that the early saints Dewi, Teilo and Illtud founded in Wales. Regrettably there are no remains or even any trace of their buildings today. Why is this, do you think?

Benedict founded a large number of monasteries in Normandy in north-east France, all of which received the support of the nobility and the king. Similarly, after defeating the English, the Normans expressed their gratitude by founding a number of monasteries in England.

G

Here are some Benedictines G. You can see why they were called 'the Black Monks'. Their close association with the invading Normans, however, made their order unpopular when they established houses in Wales.

This is what Gerald of Wales, who lived between about 1146 and 1223, has to say about the Benedictines in his book *Itinerarium Kambriae* ('The Journey Through Wales'): H

H In these houses in Gloucester and here too in Llanthony, the rule instituted by Augustine is still observed, for nowadays this order is to be preferred to all others. In its original state of poverty the Rule of St Benedict was most admirable, but later on the order accumulated immense wealth through the unstinting charity of its many benefactors ...

Gerald goes on to say how concerned the monks of Llanthony were when they found themselves being enriched by gifts of land from their lord and patron Hugh de Lacy and other godly benefactors. In their early years, because of their desire to live in poverty, they had refused many offers. In fact, they would not even allow the overgrown and wooded parts of their remote valley to be cleared and levelled in case doing so might result in their being lured away from their solitary existence. But despite their best intentions, says Gerald, 'their wealth and **endowments** rapidly accumulated'.

I Bernard of Clairvaux.

The **Cistercian** Order was founded by someone called Robert de Molesme. He and his followers believed that the Benedictines were getting slack and neglecting many of St Benedict's own rules. The mother-house of the new order was at Cîteaux, and it was monks from Clairvaux, a daughter-house of Cîteaux, where St Bernard was Abbot, who were invited to establish a monastery at Whitland.

Whitland, in turn, became the mother-house of most of the Cistercian monasteries in Wales.

Here is a picture of some Cistercians . You can see why they were known as the 'White Monks'.

J

'The Cistercians', says Professor Glanmor Williams, 'far from clinging to the skirts of castle and borough ... sought out the solitude of the mountain and moorland'. As a result they became first-rate agriculturalists, that is, farmers, shepherds, and specialists in rearing Welsh mountain sheep.

Gerald of Wales does not present an entirely flattering picture of the Cistercians, as the following excerpt shows: K

K The Cistercian Order ... broke away from the Benedictines because ... they were anxious to revive the poverty and holiness of former times ... Though the mountainsides abound in horses, the woods are well-stocked with pigs, the clearings with goats, the pastures with sheep, the meadows with cattle and the farmers with ploughs, because of our insatiable appetites each seems inadequate. And so we encroach on one another's lands, remove fences and cross boundary-lines. As a result our market places are stocked high with merchandise, while our courts of justice are kept endlessly busy with law suits and complaints ... Nevertheless, we are inclined to think that this greed arises from good intentions ... because it is in the name of hospitality that the members of this order provide charity to the poor and to wayfarers. And because they do not live on their rents as others do but by the fruits of their labour ... they anxiously seek to acquire lands ... manors and broad pastures so that they may produce enough to perform these charitable activities ... For they seem to be saying with the Gospel, 'Let us do evil that good may come'.

(Gerald of Wales, *Itinerarium Kambriae*)

This suggests that the native Welsh may have had a different opinion of the Cistercians from Gerald's. Does picture L give any indication of how they were viewed by the people of Wales?

L

4. SCENES FROM MONASTIC LIFE

THE DAILY ROUND

Look at the following timetable:

A A Monk's Winter Time-table

2.30	Rise
3.00	Night Office (service)
6.00	Prime (second service)
7.00	Study
8.00	Terce (third service)
9.00	Meeting in the chapter house
10.00	Work
12.00	Mass (Communion Service)
2.00	Dinner
3.00	Recreation
4.00	Vespers (Evensong)
5.30	Supper
7.00	Compline (last service of the day)

How many services are held in the monastery? How many hours are there for work? Using this timetable as a guide, let us look more closely at a typical day in a monastery.

At half past two in the morning the bell-ringer — the sacrist — passes through the **dormitory** ringing a small hand-bell to rouse the monks from sleep. They rise and descend the night stair to the monastery church, as in picture B.

There, in the choir of the church, they recite the psalms they have said so often they know them by heart, though keeping awake so early in the morning must be quite difficult!

Picture C shows monks reciting psalms in the choir. Are there any clues as to what time of day it is?

C Monks in the choir.

B

11

The monks may now go back to the dormitory to sleep or they may remain in the church until the next service, which will be Prime. Between seven and eight they will read or meditate in the **cloister**, until around eight when they will eat a light breakfast consisting of a slice of bread with a little wine or ale. They then return to the church for Terce, the third service.

D The chapter-house.

At nine o'clock all the brothers assemble in the **chapter-house** to meet with the abbot or prior. After prayer and hearing a lesson from the scripture, one of them will read a chapter from the rules of the monastery: this is how the chapter-house acquired its name. Then the abbot sets the monks their tasks for the day, after which he proceeds to disciplining those guilty of breaking the rules of the house. What do you think is happening in picture D? As it happens, we have a description of what took place in a chapter-house from a book written in 1075 by the archbishop of Canterbury at that time, Lanfranc: E

E The superior (i.e. the abbot) says, Let us now speak of matters of discipline ... Then the accuser states clearly whom he means to accuse ... He who is to undergo punishment shall be scourged with a single stout rod while he lies prostrate on the ground, or with a bundle of finer rods on his bare back. In each case the severity of the punishment is at the discretion of the superior.

The meeting in the chapter-house ends at ten o'clock, and for the next two hours the monks retire to the cloister to study and pursue other intellectual activities if they do not go out to work in the fields. At noon Mass is celebrated, the principal service of the day; then at two it is time for the monks to

prepare for dinner by washing their hands in a room like that in photograph F in Gloucester Cathedral. Then they enter the refectory to dine.

F Monks' wash place, a trough with running water.

You notice the difference between this and your own bathroom!

Here are some rules concerning meal times: G

G Let two cooked dishes suffice for all the brethren: and if any fruit or young vegetables are available, let a third be added. Let a good pound weight suffice for the day ... We believe that half a pint of wine is sufficient for each. At the meals of the brethren there should not fail to be reading.

Were they elaborate meals? Look at picture H to see how the refectory looked at meal times:

H

The abbot and senior brothers sit at table on a dais, or low platform, with their backs to the eastern end of the refectory. A monk reads part of scripture from the pulpit while the other brethren eat silently. Since silence is compulsory some monks have devised a sign-language to communicate with each other, like this:

Beverage   Make a gesture as if drinking while stroking the front of the ear with the other hand.

Book   Pretend to be turning the pages of a book with your right hand.

Bread   Form a circle with your thumbs and index fingers for white bread. If you require brown bread, touch the sleeve of your cowl.

Cheese   Lay the palm of your right hand flat on the left.

Clothes   Rub the tips of the fingers of your right hand up and down against the tips of the left.

Cold   Pretend to be shaking water from your hand, or blow on your index finger.

Drink   Bend your right thumb and place it on your lower lip.

Eating   Put thumb and first two fingers of your right hand to your mouth.

Fish   Make a motion with the hand in imitation of the tail-fin of a fish moving through water.

Hot   Press your index finger to your closed mouth.

Keep   Place your right hand under your left arm pit.

King   Place the tips of your fingers together on your forehead.

Man   Grasp your beard with your right hand.

Mustard   Rub your nose with the upper part of your right fist.

Saucer   Draw a circle on the palm of your left hand with the little finger of your right.

Washing   Rub the back of your left hand with the palm of your right.

If you were forced to remain silent during meal times, what signs would you use?

When they have eaten, the monks go each to his own task, some to manual work in the fields, others to stroll the walks of the monastery, and others again to study in the little cubicles known as carrels that you see on the right of picture Ⅱ. At four o'clock it is time for Evensong in church, after which a light supper of bread and a little beer is followed at seven by the last service of the day, known as Compline.

When Compline is over the brethren are probably glad to return to their dormitory after a long and hard day's activities. What would your feelings be after such a day?

Ⅱ

TASKS AND DUTIES

In order for the monastery to function properly it required a host of various officials to maintain it. The head of the house was the Abbot, whose responsibility it was to ensure discipline, organize the monastic routine, safeguard its possessions and see to it that the brothers lived according to the Rules, as the following injunction makes plain: Ⅰ

Ⅰ No monk shall have anything of his own. So the abbot sees to the clothes of each — cowl, tunic, stockings, shoes, rope girdle, knife, needle, cloths and writing tablets. The abbot is to search the beds of the monks regularly lest any private property be concealed in them. If any brother be found to have anything that he has not received from the abbot, let him undergo the strictest punishment.

Another rule advised the monks how they should behave in the presence of the abbot: K

K When he goes by, each is to stand and bow to him. None should presume to sit in the chapter-house or in the refectory until he had done so. When he sits in the cloister no-one should occupy the place next to him unless bidden. No monk should be too forward in his dealings with the abbot since he is believed to hold the place of Christ himself.

Can you explain why the abbot was given so much authority over the lives of the monks?

The abbot lived apart in his own lodgings — a building similar to that in Castle Acre abbey in Norfolk: L

L

Here is a list of the monastery's main officials: M

M

THE OFFICIALS OF THE MONASTERY

Abbot
Prior
Master of the Novices
Precentor — Cantor
Sacrist
Cellarer
Kitchener   Refectorian   Chamberlain
Choir Monks
Lay Brothers
Novices

In the abbot's absence, the responsibility for supervising the running of the monastery fell on the prior, who could therefore be regarded as the deputy-abbot.

The master of the novices prepared the young men for that time when they would be received as professed monks.

In picture N you see the precentor. He was a key official in that he was responsible for the church services, which he led from his customary position on the right hand of the choir.

The sacrist saw to the church buildings, its sacred plate, vestments and candles for the services. He had a room alongside the altar and summoned the monks to their devotions by ringing his bell at the appropriate times.

N

The cellarer, according to Lanfranc, 'should be the father of the whole community', for he bore responsibility for the corn that the monastery received from its farms and granges. He ensured there was abundant flour and beer for every meal, as well as a plentiful supply of fish, which was eaten every Friday.

Was the cellarer pictured in Ⓞ as attentive to his duties as he was expected to be according to the following rule? Ⓟ

Ⓟ [He should be] prudent, of good sense, sober, not a gluttonous eater. Let him look upon all the utensils of the monastery and its whole property as upon the sacred vessels of the altar. Let him not think that anything may be neglected ... nor be wasteful and a squanderer of the monastery's substance.

The kitchener, as his name suggests, worked in the monastery kitchen, preparing and cooking the food received from the cellarer. Another official, the refectorian, looked after the dining tables and saw that the floor was clean by throwing fresh straw down every day.

Ⓠ

When a monk fell sick like the one who is ailing in picture Ⓠ, or became too old to work, he was taken to the infirmary, where he came under the care of the infirmarian. In the infirmary the sick were given flesh-meat to enable them to recover their strength, but this was something they were not normally allowed to eat.

Ⓞ

Here is a picture of the almshouse of Evesham abbey, Ⓡ. It is built near the wall that enclosed the monastery — why, do you think?

Ⓡ

In his Rule, Benedict states that he expects the monks to take care of the poor by providing them with food, clothes and lodging. The character of the almoner and his obligations to the poor were prescribed like this: [S]

[S] The Almoner should be gentle, considerate and God-fearing ... Should he see someone without clothes, he will dress him; should he hear of anyone hungry or thirsty or of a stranger or anyone in sickness or in prison, let him, according to need, comfort him with mercy and godliness.

Travellers, too, expected to find hospitality in a monastery since there was little in the way of lodging-houses in the Middle Ages. The guest-house, like the one below [T] in Dover abbey, was built outside the monastic walls. One of the rules of St Benedict explains why: [U]

[T]

[U] Let there be a guest house set apart so that the brethren may not be disturbed when guests — who are never lacking in a monastery — arrive at irregular hours ...

It was the guest-master's responsibility to see that travellers received nourishing food and clean, comfortable beds. He rose in the morning to make sure that visitors took all their belongings with them as they resumed their journey, and to ensure also that they did not remove table-linen, cloths and towels belonging to the monastery.

[V]

Finally we come to the chamberlain. Picture [V] shows him talking to some of his assistants. His responsibility was to ensure every monk had garments and new footwear as required. Every year he laid fresh straw on every mattress in each bed in the dormitory and kept the wash-room in the cloister tidy. The monks washed and shaved every day, and trimmed their tonsures every three weeks to keep their pates bald. On these occasions the chamberlain saw to it that there was plenty of hot water and dry clothes at the monks' disposal.

5. MONASTIC ESTATES AND POSSESSIONS

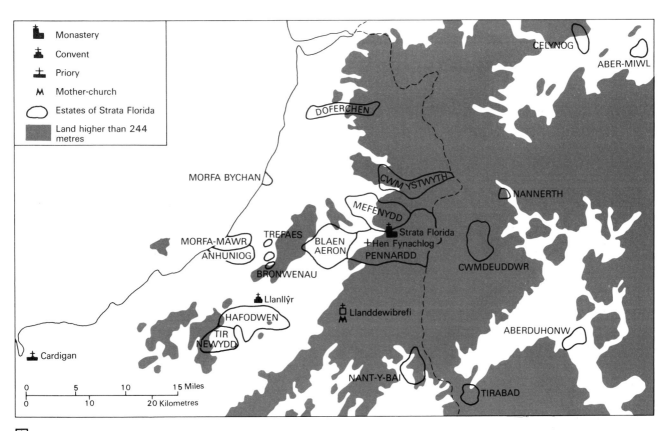

Map legend:
- Monastery
- Convent
- Priory
- M Mother-church
- Estates of Strata Florida
- Land higher than 244 metres

Map labels: CELYNOG, ABER-MIWL, DOFERCHEN, MORFA BYCHAN, CWM YSTWYTH, NANNERTH, MEFENYDD, TREFAES, MORFA-MAWR, BLAEN AERON, Strata Florida, Hen Fynachlog, ANHUNIOG, PENNARDD, CWMDEUDDWR, BRONWENAU, Llanllŷr, HAFODWEN, Llanddewibrefi, TIR NEWYDD, ABERDUHONW, Cardigan, NANT-Y-BAI, TIRABAD

Scale: 0 5 10 15 Miles / 0 10 20 Kilometres

A

The Welsh monasteries received the patronage of both Norman earls and Welsh princes. The principal aim of a **patron** was to provide land on which a monastery might be built and where a community of monks could support itself. When a donor made a grant to found a monastery in this way his intention was to provide not only lands but what were known as 'spiritual possessions' as well. Here are the details (dating from between 1115 and 1130) of a grant by Gilbert de Clare to the monastery of Llanbadarn which give some indication of what this might involve: **B**

B Grant by Gilbert, son of Richard, for the souls of his lord, King Henry, his son and his parents, to the monastery of St Peters, Gloucester, to build a priory at Llanbadarn in South Wales, of the church of St Padarn and all things which belong to it, between the bounds of the sea and the two rivers as he has perambulated it, also half of the great fishery with other fisheries, mills, meadows, pastures, woods and groves and all other things belonging to that church in pure and perpetual alms ... retaining nothing for himself save only prayers by the monks serving in that priory. He grants also all taxes from all chapels belonging to St Padarn, the offerings brought to the altar of his chapel in his castle, so that the prior and monks of St Padarn shall possess for ever, without any custom and demand, the land which is between the Rheidol and the Clarach from the sea to the ditch of St Padarn, and so running by the land which is

called the land of Wymund de St Audeon to Clarach, and the whole water which is between him and the monks to fish. He gives also to them the church of Cardigan with all its appurtenances. He and his successors will defend all these gifts for ever, against all men ...

So a patron donated land on which a monastery could be built and where the monks could support themselves by farming and stock-rearing. Whether the land was arable or pasture depended on the location of the monastery, which depended in turn on the kind of land owned by the donor. The grant might also contain rights to build a mill, fisheries and orchards and to receive the gifts in kind of the local inhabitants.

Map **A** shows the location of the various landed estates owned by the monastery of Strata Florida.

It shows you that Strata Florida owned many lands in mid-Wales. Draw up a list of them. While gardens, orchards and its own farm lands lay around the monastery, its other estates were given to tenants who paid rent from their produce. Some of these worked part-time on the monastery's own farm, while the tenants of Doferchen were expected to carry iron and salt to Strata Florida from Aberystwyth, fifteen miles away. Similarly, it was an obligation upon the tenants of Cwm Ystwyth to convey building materials to repair the outer fabric of the monastery.

The monasteries that were founded in Wales soon became major landowners in their own right. Table C shows rough estimates of the acreage of land owned by some monasteries. How does their size compare with a typical Welsh upland farm of today?

C

Monastery	Arable (i.e. cultivated) land in acres	Pasture (i.e. grazing) land in acres	Total
Cwm-hir	3,000		3,000
Grace Dieu	1,800		1,800
Margam	6,420	517	6,937
Neath	4,883	325	5,208
Strata Florida	6,360		6,360
Tintern	3,048	165	3,213
Whitland	5,040		5,040

The size of their estates and the large number of animals they reared on them enabled the monasteries to provide work on the land for entire villages. As an example, table D shows the approximate number of sheep owned by certain abbeys in south Wales in 1291. Did Gerald of Wales have some grounds for complaint after all, perhaps?

D

Monastery	Number of sheep
Cwm-hir	300
Grace Dieu	22
Margam	5,245
Neath	4,897
Strata Florida	1,327
Tintern	3,264
Whitland	1,100

Other kinds of property were the 'spiritual possessions', as they were called, that is, the **tithe** and other parish dues paid to the priest for his upkeep. Once again, Gerald of Wales had some harsh things to say about the monasteries' eagerness to get their hands on 'spiritual possessions': E

E It is wonderful how all the houses of this order [Cistercian] almost throughout the whole of Wales are contaminated by the infectious vice of avarice. For they recklessly take possession of churches by occupying parts of parishes: many, too, they presume to ruin and utterly destroy by a wholesale purchase of their lands, expelling the very cultavitors themselves.

(Gerald of Wales, *Speculum Ecclesiae*, about 1217)

Here is an example of a church and its spiritual posessions ('means') being made over as a gift to Valle Crucis abbey: F

F Reyner, Bishop of St Asaph, left to the Abbot and Monastery of Valle Crucis the means of the church of Wrexham for the building of his church ... dated May 1220 ... Confirmation by Abraham, Bishop of St Asaph, in the year 1228. The Bishop left to the same Abbot and Monastery other means of a church in Wrexham in the year 1227. Confirmation ... by the Archbishop of Canterbury of the leaving of the whole church of Wrexham to that same Abbot and Monastery, by Abraham, Bishop of St Asaph.

(Translated from the *Red Book of Asaph*)

Careful study of this and similar documents tells us that the monastery at Valle Crucis owned the rectories and churches of Wrexham, Ruabon, Llangollen, Chirk, Llansantffraid, Llantisilio and Bryneglwys. In 1535 the tithes of these churches were worth £141 *per annum*, a sum considerably in excess of the £47 the monastery made from tilling the soil and sheep-rearing. Table G shows the profits made by some monastic houses in 1291.

G

Monastery	Profits from farming	Profits from churches	Total
Cwm-hir	£35.60	—	£35.60
Grace Dieu	£18.28	—	£18.28
Margam	£255.37	0.50p	£255.87
Neath	£231.07	£5.00	£236.07
Strata Florida	£82.34	£16.00	£98.34
Tintern	£108.48	£36.67	£145.15
Whitland	£43.77	—	£43.77

With the help of the information provided earlier in tables C and D, try and explain some of these figures in G above.

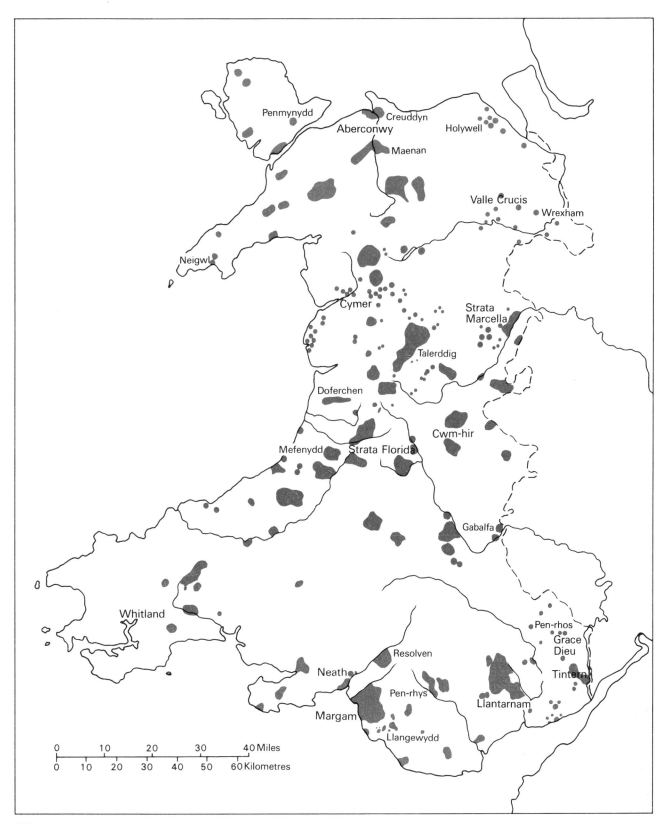

Penmynydd

Creuddyn
Aberconwy
Holywell
Maenan

Valle Crucis
Wrexham

Neigwl

Cymer
Strata
Marcella

Talerddig

Doferchen

Cwm-hir

Mefenydd Strata Florida

Gabalfa

Whitland

Pen-rhos
Grace
Dieu
Resolven
Neath
Tintern
Pen-rhys
Margam Llantarnam

Llangewydd

| 0 | 10 | 20 | 30 | 40 Miles |
| 0 | 10 | 20 | 30 | 40 | 50 | 60 Kilometres |

H Cistercian Lands in Wales.

6. THE TURNING OF THE TIDE

A

Here are the ruins of Valle Crucis abbey A. You cannot help noticing the caravan site in the background! Bearing in mind the splendid history of the monastic houses — their importance, their extensive buildings and broad, widely-dispersed estates in the Middle Ages — how did such a reversal of fortune come about?

The decline of the Welsh monasteries probably began during the Revolt of Owain Glyndŵr (1399–1416). Owain was supported by most of the abbeys that were of Welsh foundation (see p.7). Among those that backed him from the very beginning were the abbeys at Aberconwy, Strata Florida, Whitland and Llantarnam. The abbot of Llantarnam, John ap Hywel, was actually killed fighting for Glyndŵr at the battle of Pwll Melyn, near Usk, in 1405. Henry IV's army desecrated Aberconwy abbey in 1400, plundering its books, vestments and treasure before setting the entire building alight.

Adam of Usk describes what happened at Strata Florida during Henry IV's first campaign in Wales in 1402: B

B That autumn, with all north Wales, Ceredigion and Powys supporting ... Owain Glyndŵr ... the English invaded those parts in great force, utterly laying them waste with fire, famine and sword, not sparing even children or churches, nor the monastery at Strata Florida in which the king himself was received as guest. Its church and choir right up to the high altar they used as a stable ... and carried away with them into England over a thousand children of both sexes to be their servants.

But it was not only the royal armies that vandalised Welsh monasteries. Adam of Usk also relates that Owain Glyndŵr's men descended on the bishopric of Llandaff: C

C ... like the Assyrian ... committing deeds of unheard of cruelty with sword and fire.

During the Rebellion Owain Glyndŵr's men took full revenge on those monasteries that supported the English. The abbeys of Ewenni and Cardiff suffered heavily; when theirs was destroyed by the rebels, the monks of Llanthony sought refuge in Hereford. And even though the abbey of Cwm-hir was the burial-place of Llywelyn the Last, it was still sacked by Glyndŵr's men because the abbot had sided with the English. By 1410 the abbey at Talley had D

D ... by frequent incursions of men at arms [of both sides] been despoiled, burned and almost destroyed ...

(Calendar of Papal Letters, vi, 230-1)

By the beginning of the sixteenth century many of the Welsh monasteries were in a sorry state indeed. Few monks now lived the good and pious lives expected of them. The Welsh poet Guto'r Glyn in the fifteenth century was lavish in his praise of the generosity of the abbot of Shrewsbury at whose well-laid table, groaning under all kinds of foods and wines, he had eaten enough to last him a month. From this, and from the cellarer pictured in E, what impression do you get of monastic life by the fifteenth century?

Earlier in the Middle Ages Gerald of Wales had already written critically of the monks (see p.10), and here is a stern rebuke issued to the Cistercians by a contemporary English poet: F

 F

Livings and churches they buy
And many ways to cheat they try
They buy and sell at profit
Awaiting settling day.
And well they sell their corn
And I have heard they do not scorn
To lend their money to the Jews.

(quoted by Marjorie Rowling in *Everyday Life in Medieval Times*)

Henry VIII (1509-47) saw a way of silencing the grievances and grudges his subjects harboured against the monasteries by bringing about their dissolution. In this way their immense wealth would be transferred to the Crown. In 1535 he sent out commissioners to inquire into and estimate the annual income of every monastic house in England and Wales, and the details were collected together in a bulky volume known as the *Valor Ecclesiasticus*. Professor Glanmor Williams has described it as 'that extraordinary Domesday Book of the Church', and among its findings was the fact that not one monastery in Wales had an income of £200 a year.

The first commission was followed a few months later by a second. This time the commissioners were instructed to look for monastic abuses so that the decision that had already been taken to confiscate and seize the wealth and possessions of the monasteries could then be justified.

A team of three — Dr John Vaughan, Dr Adam Becansaw and Ellis Price — came to investigate the condition of the Welsh monastic houses. Evidence of scandalous living was not difficult to come by. In the course of their inquiries into Valle Crucis abbey, for example, it was revealed that the abbot, Robert Salisbury, was the ring-leader of a band of highway robbers in Oxfordshire. This is the evidence of a contemporary letter: G

G Sent to Oxford to seize the Abbot ... The Abbot is abbot of Valle Crucis, in Wales, and is a White Monk named Sallysbere [Salisbury] ... They have committed many robberies.

The abbot was arrested and imprisoned in the course of the investigation of his monastery by John Vaughan and Adam Becansaw in August 1535. The commissioners reported that the abbey contained only six monks, only one of whom — 'a good, virtuous and well-disposed man' — was of sufficient character to become abbot, but this was unlikely to happen 'considering the said house to be already far in debt and decay'.

The English monastic houses were discovered to be in no better condition. This is an excerpt from the evidence brought by the royal commissioners against Peterborough abbey: H

H The abbot's brother lives splendidly on the revenues of the Abbey. Nor does the abbot choose dutiful monks but gives preference to indolent ones. There is a tavern within the Abbey where the brethren drink freely. The abbot retains for his own use the money he makes from selling the livestock that belongs to the house ... The sacrist lives with a woman called Joan Turner.

Such extreme cases as these were exceptional, however. The commissioners found that the majority of the monks were harmless enough, but the government was determined to push ahead with its scheme to suppress the monasteries. In 1536 every abbey with an income of less than £200 was closed down, and by 1539 every single monastic house in England and Wales had been dissolved.

Table **I** shows the profit made by the Crown within ten years of the dissolution of the monasteries.

I

Revenues from monastic lands	£415,505
Profit after selling off the lands	£855,711
Profit after selling off monastic buildings, bells and lead	£26,502
Profit after selling off monastic silver and gold plate	£79,081

Over the centuries the monasteries had acquired many treasurers and valuable possessions, like those shown in **J**. Now they all became the property of the Crown.

In picture **K** the royal commissioners are seen interrogating an abbot, while some of the abbey's valuables lie on the table between them.

J

K

So what happened to the monks? Most of them received an annual pension of £5, roughly the equivalent of the income of a humble parish priest. Some abbots received very generous pensions; the abbot of Fountains Abbey in Yorkshire received £100 a year. Several monks became priests, while others went home to their families and took up work of a non-religious kind. The evidence suggests that some 1,800 out of 9,000 suffered real hardship; refused even a penny's pension, they were forced to go begging. The less fortunate among them were harried and hounded and even imprisoned for a time. Ⓛ

Once they had been dissolved, the monasteries were plundered and despoiled. Their stone, lead and timber were taken away and used to build mansions and palaces. What Shakespeare described as 'bare, ruin'd choirs' — like those of Rievaulx (Yorkshire) in Ⓜ — remain to this day to remind us of the time when the monasteries were at their peak in the Middle Ages, before they were destroyed by Henry VIII.

Ⓛ

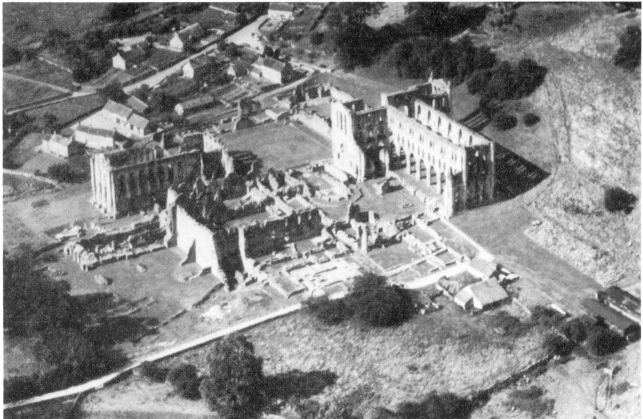

Ⓜ

Here are the words of an eye-witness who saw the break-up of Roche abbey on the borders of Yorkshire and Nottinghamshire Ⓝ

Ⓝ It would have made a heart of flint melt and weep to have seen the breaking up of the House, the sorrowful departing of the brethren and the sudden destruction that fell the same day as their departure from their home ... Nothing was spared save the cowsheds, pigsties and such other pens as stood outside the walls.

What do *you* think of the fate of the monasteries?

7. GLOSSARY

Abbey — a building occupied by monks under the headship of an abbot.

Benedictines (The Black Monks) — an order of monks living according to the rule of St Benedict.

Chapter-house — a building in a monastery where the monastic community assembled daily for a general meeting.

Cistercians (The White Monks) — an order of monks founded in 1098 at Cistercium or Cîteaux, a stricter offshoot of the Benedictines.

Cloister — a covered walk around the central quadrangle of a monastery where the monks retired to read and meditate.

Dormitory — the monks' sleeping quarters.

Endowment — property which has been provided for the use of a monastery or church.

Hermit — a person who has chosen for religious reasons to withdraw from the world to live in solitude.

Monk — a member of a community of men living apart from the world under religius vows.

Monastery — the house of a community of monks.

Novice — a member of a monastic community under training who has not yet taken vows.

Nun — a member of a community of women living apart from the world under religious vows.

Patron — one who provides land and money for the founding of a monastery.

Refectory — the monks' dining room.

Tithe — a tax paid to the church in the form of the tenth part of the annual produce of land.

Tonsure — the part of a monk's head left bare after it has been shaved as a preparation for admission to a monastic order.

Walk — a place set apart for walking in the monastery, such as a cloister.